Get Out of That, Then!

Get Out of That, Then!

Scenes to perform, read and tape

Lucy Parker and Tony Grounds
A Shiftwork company script

Edward Arnold

First published 1984 by
Edward Arnold (Publishers) Ltd
41 Bedford Square
London WC1B 3DQ

British Library Cataloguing in Publication Data

Parker, Lucy
Get out of that, then!
I. Title II. Grounds, Tony
822'.914 PR6066.A6/

ISBN 0-7131-7298-3

The Authors wish to thank the Lyric Theatre, Hammersmith for its help and co-operation.

SHIFT
WORK

A Shiftwork script

Text set in 11 point Linoterm Palatino by
The Castlefield Press, Moulton, Northants.
Printed in Great Britain

Contents

Introduction

1 Using the book

Get Out of That, Then! was presented as a whole production and can be used as such or as a collection of scenes linked by a common theme. Each scene stands on its own. You may want to use the scripts to perform, read or tape.

At the back of the book, there are suggestions for warm-up exercises to encourage discussion or drama work before beginning on the material itself.

There are also ideas for follow-up work after each script which are intended to be a resource to use however best suits your needs. They cover drama, written and discussion work to prompt the groups which use *Get Out of That, Then!* into further activity of their own. You may want to build an extensive series of sessions around one scene or to look at several, making the connection between them as you go.

2 Background

A single thread unites the scenes in *Get Out of That, Then!* They are all about the relationship of one person to the crowd. Each individual is inevitably on his or her own – each wants a secret, separate identity; his or her concerns are no one else's and in the end no one else can really help that person. Yet, at the same time, no one really wants to be all alone – each of us wants friends and wants to be part of the swirling mass of people around. Look, for example, at the monologues. In '9.38' David is trapped in the isolation of his own room. But, still he imagines 'thousands and thousands of people' alone, each feeling the same way. Jackie's monologue is about being spotted for a moment in a crowd. In the scene where Diannah cries for her mother, she must of course get our sympathy and Eddie is cruel for making fun of her. But Eddie gets the last word; what can *he* do about *her* problems? There's you – and then there's everyone else.

In performance, there was a crowd on stage. The cast was twenty-one strong and all of them were on all the time. So each scene was set against a mass of people. For a moment someone surfaced from the crowd to tell their story, to perform their scene . . . only to be pulled back in again – for someone else to emerge. In rehearsal we came to call this crowd 'The Heap'.

The play began and ended with 'The Heap' – everyone struggling to be heard above the others. And so we ended on the note on which we began. However, there was a development in the tone of the scenes. I think of it as an octave – the same note but a different pitch. In 'The Diary' those secret thoughts of Giselle's are hidden, to be protected from a hostile world which wants to snatch them and does not understand them. Early on in the play came those scenes where a person is fighting to make an identity apart. Later came the scenes with questions left in the air and the efforts to make connections with other people. At the end, Giselle offers her diary to a friend to read . . . a gesture towards a more mellow balance in the relationship between one person and the crowd around her.

3 How the play was created

These scenes originated through improvisation, discussion and subsequent performance by Shiftwork—the youth company at the Lyric Theatre, Hammersmith. The characters, situations and dialogue are really those of the actors.

The company was auditioned from all those who arrived in answer to advertisements, which went out to schools, colleges, papers and radio stations. There were about two dozen in the group: some had done drama work in school but many had done nothing like this at all before.

We worked together for six weeks, meeting three times a week, in evenings and on Sundays to come up with the ideas. Gradually, the theme developed and all the improvisations were taped. Then, Tony Grounds disappeared for a few weeks under a mountain of material – and emerged with the finished scenes, shaped from the original improvisations.

To create the material, the group drew on their own lives. Giselle's diary is real. The relationship between Richard and Gary exists. The indistinct history of herself which Joyce confides in us, is true . . .

In those initial workshops in which the show was invented, it was important to everyone that when Mick talked about being a postman, he was a postman. And for other people, working later with a script which was created in this way, one of the exciting things is knowing that someone did first express that feeling for themselves; the origin of the part came from the actual experience of that person. If it is convincing it is because of this sense of reality which is built into it.

4 Mounting a production

In production 'the Heap' was a short dramatic sequence which opened and closed the show. Here it is put at the back of the book, in case you should wish to go directly to reading the scenes rather than performing them.

If you go on to make your own production you may want to bear in mind the order in which we used the scenes. 'Can You Hear Me?' was at the start, coming straight out of 'the Heap', where people were shouting at one another to try and make contact. The first major scenes were 'The Diary' followed by 'Richard on the Floor', both about individuals under an aggressive attack. Then 'Diannah', 'A Birthday' and 'The Promotion' which posed a lot of questions about how close or separate people can be. Finally, it moved on to friends deciding to share something of themselves at the end of 'Natalie Wood' and then in 'Giselle's Diary'. The monologues were interspersed through the production, like punctuation marks. They are short and swift, summing up a lot of the ideas in the scenes.

Lucy Parker

The Diary

Giselle **Sharon** **Madeleine**
Colin **Alfie**

At Alfie's home. **Giselle** *is writing her diary. From the other side of the room,* **Madeleine** *watches her intently.* **Sharon** *is reading.* **Alfie** *and* **Colin** *are larking about. To begin with it is almost as though there are two scenes.* **Alfie** *and* **Colin** *dominate the activity with their noise and games. Meanwhile, there is an undercurrent of tension created by the way* **Madeleine** *stares at* **Giselle**. *Everyone is engrossed in what they are doing for a little while before there is any dialogue.*

Giselle (*thinking about her diary but talking outloud to herself*) What did we do yesterday?
Madeleine Doing your diary again, are you?
Giselle Yeah.
Madeleine (*sarcastically*) The whole truth and nothing but the truth?
Alfie (*to* **Colin**) Yeah, what did we do yesterday?
Sharon What's wrong Madeleine? You look upset.
(**Alfie** *and* **Colin** *are making a lot of noise.*)
Madeleine Nothing. Really.
Sharon (*to* **Alfie** *and* **Colin**) You're kids you two.
Alfie What's wrong with that, eh?
Madeleine Yeah, what were we doing yesterday? We were going to meet Adam, weren't we?
Giselle Oh yes. That's right.
Colin He's alright Adam, you know.
Giselle I don't want to be rude, but I think he's a burk.
Madeleine Yes, you do, don't you. You think he's a real burk.
Giselle Yeah, I do. I told you.
Madeleine I expect you even hate his guts.
Giselle Umm? . . . Yes, I expect I do.
Madeleine Liar!
Giselle What do you mean liar?
Madeleine Bitch!
Madeleine What do you mean bitch?
Alfie (*jokingly*) Give this lady a dictionary.

Madeleine (*still to* **Giselle**) Think about it, okay.
Giselle What do you mean 'think about it'?
Madeleine It's right in front of you.
Colin Can you two let us in on this?
Sharon What's the matter, Madeleine?
Giselle (*the penny drops*) Wait a minute. Have you been looking somewhere you shouldn't?
Alfie and Colin (*together*) Ooooh!
Madeleine Maybe.
Giselle What do you mean, maybe? I said, have you been looking somewhere you shouldn't?
Madeleine Yes. I have.
Giselle What do you mean, you have? (*pause*) You've been reading my diary, haven't you.

Suddenly the problem is clear. **Alfie** *and* **Colin** *are delighted at the prospect of a good argument. For a while they send up the fight, watching it as if it were a tennis match.*

Madeleine It was just . . . sort of . . .
Giselle It was just sort of . . . what?
Madeleine There!
Giselle Well, you keep your nose out of my diary!
Sharon (*to* **Madeleine**) You know she never leaves her diary around. She's paranoid about it.
Giselle It was in my drawer, so you've been going through my room. You leave my drawer alone! It's my own personal property. You don't touch it!
Madeleine Yeah, well, you leave my fella alone.
Giselle I don't want to touch your fella.
Madeleine Yes, you do. It's what it says in your diary, sugar. (**Alfie** *and* **Colin** *giggle. The plot has thickened.*)
Giselle Well, you wouldn't have known, if you hadn't read it, would you?
Madeleine Well, I have read it and now I do know.
Giselle I don't care if you do know. You leave my diary alone. What I write in there is me, what is on those pages is me and it's got nothing to do with you.
Madeleine It has got something to do with me.
Giselle It's my private property!

Madeleine He's my private property, so you keep off him. I'm glad I found out. You go near him and I'll slit your throat, bitch.

Sharon Madeleine!

Colin Cool it. (*He goes up to her, offering her some of the drink he has been having.*) Here, have a drink.

Madeleine I don't want a drink.

Colin Look, it's only a diary.

Madeleine Yes. It's only a diary. And he's only my boyfriend.

(*She pushes* **Colin's** *arm and the drink spills.*)

Alfie Hey! Spilling drink all over the carpet. My mum'll kill me, man.

Madeleine I don't give a toss about your mum . . . 'man'.

Giselle You just tell her to leave my diary alone.

Madeleine You tell her to leave my fella alone.

Giselle Stop shouting.

Madeleine I thought you were my friend. My best friend.

Sharon I'll tell you what Madeleine. I wouldn't touch your boyfriend with a disinfected barge-pole.

Madeleine Good. Maybe you'rė a better friend than her.

(**Alfie** *is on his hands and knees trying to scrub the stain out of the carpet.*)

Colin Will it come out?

Alfie All over the carpet. All over the bloody carpet. All over my mum's bloody carpet!

Sharon What have you written about me in there?

Giselle I haven't written anything about you in there. And if I had, it'd have nothing to do with you.

Madeleine I bet you haven't written anything about her. I bet you haven't written anything about Alfie and Colin either.

Giselle Well, I'm allowed to if I want. I'm allowed to have thoughts. I expect even you have them too.

Madeleine You have lots of thoughts.

Giselle Yes. And I write them down.

Sharon She can't help it if she fancies him.

Madeleine She can help making little plots.

Giselle If your boyfriend is so faithful, my plots won't make any difference will they?

Madeleine It's not whether he's faithful or not. It's my friend making plots.

Giselle Madeleine, I haven't laid a hand on your

boyfriend. You *took* my diary and I don't like that.

Madeleine Okay, so we don't like each other.

Giselle I never said that.

(**Colin** *goes across to comfort* **Madeleine**.)

Colin Come on, calm down.

Giselle Oi! What are you crawling to her for? She read my diary.

(**Colin** *turns to* **Giselle**) No, I don't want to be crawled to second.

Colin I'm not crawling.

Alfie (*taking the mickey*) Crawler Colin!

Colin You just clean the carpet or your mummy will send you be bed with no tea. Look, Madeleine, so what if she fancies your bloke. It's a compliment. And you'd be really peeved if she found him ugly.

Madeleine Oh yeah?

Alfie Right now, everyone, calm down.

Giselle No, I won't. It's not fair.

Alfie Look, my mum will be coming home soon.

Giselle It's not fair. You know how much my diary means to me.

Madeleine And Adam to me.

Sharon Madeleine, what's more important to you? Your fella or your friendship?

Giselle What I put in there, well, it's me. Everything in here is my feelings, my thoughts. This isn't for other people to read.

Madeleine You sit around all the time writing that blessed diary.

Giselle That's what you're jealous of, isn't it? You're jealous of my diary.

Colin I don't understand your diary.

Giselle (*to* **Colin**) You don't have to understand it. If you don't like it, you can just lump it.

Alfie Why do you write a diary?

Giselle Because . . .

Madeleine So she can write her secrets.

Giselle Because there are some things I can't tell people. Some things I don't want to tell people. There are parts of me I don't want to show people.

Colin Madeleine, do you write a diary?

Madeleine No!

Giselle You've just read my mind. And I don't want you to. Because what goes on in my mind is mine. It's not yours and it's not his (*she points at* **Alfie**, **Colin** *and* **Sharon** *in turn*) – or his or hers, it's mine. It's not yours to snoop in.

Colin If these things are so personal, you shouldn't put them in in the first place.

Giselle But there's no-one I can tell them to. Have you ever felt that you were longing to tell someone something? It is on the tip of your tongue but you couldn't say it?

(**Colin** *and* **Alfie** *laugh.*)

Alfie Yeah, that bird down the pub!

Sharon And you write it in there?

Colin (*triumphant*) Therefore . . . the only reason you write it in there is so someone can read it.

Giselle I don't want anyone to read it.

Alfie If she's dying to tell someone something, why does she write it in there?

Sharon (*pointing at* **Madeleine**) You're a naughty girl.

Giselle How it started, right, was the things I couldn't tell my mum, I wrote in my diary and it moved on from there.

Alfie You know what I believe, I believe you wanted him to know.

Giselle Wanted him to know what?

Alfie I believe you wanted him to find out.

Giselle I didn't. Just shut up.

Colin Are you going to become famous or something for doing this?

Giselle If people knew what was in here, that would be me.

Alfie Well, why do it you bloody well write it out in front of the lot of us then?

(*He tries to snatch the diary from her hand.*)

Giselle The fact that I write a diary is not secret. I've never kept that a secret from anyone. It's what's inside that's secret – like a person.

Madeleine Look, leave her. It's me who's in the wrong.

Sharon We do have a turn about!

Giselle Did she really say that?

Alfie Yeah. She's alright really. She just hangs onto her bloke like a leach.

(*Pause.*)

Colin Giselle, have you ever come across anybody else's diary?

Giselle Yeah, I have.

Colin And have you ever been tempted to read it?

Giselle No.

Alfie You haven't?

Giselle I was tempted but I didn't.

Alfie (*in disbelief*) Huh!

Sharon (*to* **Alfie**) We're not all as nosey as you, key-hole Joe.

Alfie It's not being nosey, right, it's not. But if I saw a diary there, right where that stain is, (*he points to the mark on the carpet where he has been scrubbing*) okay, I'd say 'aye-aye, I don't want to read it . . . I don't want to read it . . . .'

Sharon Then you'd sneak off to the bog with it.

Alfie (*miming grabbing the diary off the floor and running off with it*) It's natural.

Giselle Alfie! Alfie!

(*As she calls out his name a second time, she holds out her diary towards* **Alfie**, *offering it to him.*)

Ideas for development

1 The scene ends with Giselle challenging Alfie to read her diary. What happens next? Try two or three different possibilities.

2 Write Giselle's account of the events which happen in the scene, for her diary.

3 Sharon says, 'What's more important to you, your fella or your friendship?' Create a scene where someone is caught between loyalty to a boyfriend or girlfriend and a friend.

4 What do you think are the plots that Giselle came up with?

5 Suppose Giselle had not kept secret how she felt about Adam. Improvise the scene in which she tells Madeleine.

6 Alfie's main concern seems to be to keep the peace because they are in his mother's house.
   (i) Set up the scene again and have Alfie's mum come in towards the end. What happens?
   (ii) Create a situation where an incident occurs with a group of friends in one of their homes. That character must try to control the action because it is his or her parent's house.

7 Set up a scene with Alfie and Colin describing this scene to friends later.

8 Giselle blames Madeleine for reading her diary.
Madeleine blames Giselle for her secrecy.
Where do you think the blame lies?

9 Giselle says about her diary, 'It's what's inside that's secret – like a person'. Do you agree with Alfie and Colin that she really wants to share her thoughts? Or do you think that there will always be a bit of Giselle – or anyone – which is secret?

N.B. Giselle and her diary also appear at the end of this book. It may therefore be useful to look at that scene now too.

Diannah

Diannah **Peter** **Eddie**
Linda **Kate**

Everyone has been up all night at a party. **Eddie, Peter** *and* **Linda** *came along together, as did* **Diannah** *and* **Kate**. *Now they are all in limbo – waiting to be able to go home. They are slow moving, tired and uncomfortable. Although* **Diannah** *does not speak for a long time, her presence is important. She is huddled and miserable on the floor, paying no attention to anyone else.*

Eddie Eh, Peter.
Peter What?
Eddie Got the time?
Peter No.
Eddie What time do the tubes start running round here?
Kate About six.
Eddie Streuth!
Kate God, I'm so tired.

(*Pause.*)

Eddie Eh, Peter.
Peter What?
Eddie Has she gone?
Peter Yeah.
Eddie You mean you let her go?
Linda Who?
Peter She went about three in a minicab.
Linda Who? . . . I might as well talk to myself.
Eddie You shouldn't have let her go.
Kate (*to herself*) When I get home I'm going to have a bath, then straight into bed . . .
Eddie (*to* **Peter**) Don't look at me like that. What's the matter? What have I done?
Linda What's the matter, Peter?
Peter Nothing's the matter. This guy's trying to ruin my life that's all.

Eddie Oh come on, Peter. We're not going to go through this whole scene again are we?

Linda Are you two on about the bird with the blond hair? (**Eddie** *laughs.*)

Peter Why have you always got to laugh, Eddie?

Linda I thought she was quite nice.

Peter Always got to laugh.

Eddie I thought it was funny. (*He laughs again.*) I'm sorry, I'm sorry! I found it funny, right.

Peter Yeah.

Kate (*She goes up to* **Diannah**, *sitting on the floor.*) What's the matter with you?

Diannah Nothing.

Kate Well, why are you all crumpled on the floor? You look ill.

Diannah I'm alright.

Kate Come on, Diannah, let's go.

Eddie (*to* **Kate**) Your mate's upset.

Kate (*Angrily, to* **Eddie** *about* **Peter**) So's yours.

(*Pause.*)

Linda I wish there was some food here. (*Silence.* **Eddie** *laughs again.*)

Peter Shut up.

Linda What's so funny? Is it about the girl with the blond hair again?

Eddie Well, he didn't do anything.

Linda Because you were laughing at him.

Kate Why?

Eddie Well, he was looking at her, right, and she was looking at him . . .

Linda So they were looking at each other.

Kate Well, that doesn't sound all that funny to me.

Eddie For ten minutes!

Kate Well, if they want to stare at each other, why can't they?

Eddie That's fine by me. But you should have seen the way they were staring. (*He makes moon eyes . . . and laughs.*)

Kate What did you do then?

Eddie I laughed.

Linda Well, why's he so cut up about it?

(**Eddie** *shrugs.*)

Kate It seems like everyone's got problems.

Eddie That music's getting on my nerves.

Kate (*Indicating another room, where the dancing has been.*) There's hardly anyone left in there. You could play football in there, you know.

(**Peter** *has been staring balefully at* **Eddie.**)

Eddie Look, Pete, don't go blaming me, alright. Why didn't you just go up to her and ask her to dance if that's what you wanted, you idiot!

Peter Because you were bleeding laughing, that's why.

Eddie Oh come on, for ten minutes, Pete! You were looking at the girl for ten minutes. That's what I call funny.

Peter So?

Eddie All it takes is ten seconds.

Kate Oh yes? I haven't noticed with you.

Eddie (*suddenly posing*) What's your phone number, woman?

Kate You what?

Peter (*It is his turn to laugh*) She doesn't want to give you her phone number.

Kate I didn't say that, and I don't think it's funny.

Peter I think it's funny. I think it's brilliant.

(*He giggles to himself. Pause.*)

Kate Come on, Di.

Eddie Why doesn't she go home, instead of moping on the floor.

Linda She got kicked out of her home.

Kate Thrown out by her mum.

Eddie Why did you get thrown out?

Diannah It was a choice between me and my mum's boyfriend. And she chose her boyfriend. That's fair enough.

Kate You're her kid, Diannah.

Eddie Wait, you must have done something for her to chuck you out.

Linda It's just the way she is.

Kate You can't say that. You can't just say, 'that's the way she is'.

Linda Why not? I can't see any other reason.

Peter So where are you staying, Diannah?

Diannah Anywhere and everywhere.

Eddie Oh yeah? (*He laughs.*)

Kate Don't be disgusting, Eddie. Everything's funny to you, isn't it?
Peter He's a real joker.
Linda Anything you can't handle, you laugh at.
Eddie What do you want me to do, cry?

(*Pause.*)

Peter Any cornflakes?
Kate No milk.
Linda There's yoghurt. We could water it down and take the lumps out . . . that's like milk.
Eddie Any coffee?
Kate No.
Eddie Teach me to come to these rural parties (*he laughs*).
Linda He's at it again.
Eddie (*Suddenly angry at being under attack*) If I find a situation funny, I laugh. What do you want me to do?
Kate You were ridiculing Peter earlier on.
Eddie I was not ridiculing Peter.
Kate And now you're ridiculing Diannah.
Eddie I'm not ridiculing Diannah. I mean how stupid. She's been chucked out . . . so what?
Kate (*Furious*) What do you mean 'so what'?
Eddie (*Spelling out the repetition slowly*) So what? What does it matter to me, how does it affect my life? Come to think of it, how does it affect yours, you idiots.
Linda Maybe he doesn't care about anyone.
Kate Well, just one person. Himself.
Eddie And if everyone had the same attitude the world'd get on fine – no wars, nothing!
Peter You can't deal with anything, Eddie.
Eddie Of course I can. I can deal with anything. I just deal with it in a different way from the way you deal with anything.
Linda You just push it aside. Laugh it off.
Eddie And that's not dealing with it?
Peter Nah!
Eddie So what do you call dealing with it?
Peter I don't know. All I know is laughing isn't going to help.

Eddie All I know is you're not really going to help, are you? I mean, what can you really do? So where's the difference, eh? Try and tell me that.

Linda He don't hurt. You do.

Eddie Who do I hurt?

Linda You hurt Peter when you were laughing at him, and Diannah when you were laughing at her.

Eddie Look, all I'm saying is, I think it's up to whoever's concerned to buck themselves up and do something about the situation. If they don't they shouldn't blame me for laughing at their stupidity. (*He goes right up to* **Diannah**.) Excuse me, Diannah, are you hurt? Are you hurt because I laughed at you?

Diannah You do what you want to do.

Eddie The horse's mouth. You don't like your logic being thrown back in your faces, eh?

Diannah Why were you laughing anyway?

Eddie Because I felt like laughing.

Diannah What did you find funny?

Eddie What?

Diannah What did you find funny?

Eddie I just felt like laughing.

Diannah You must have found something funny.

Eddie I just laughed. I feel like laughing now. (*He laughs.*)

Diannah What's the reason now?

Eddie Because you're all looking at me with your mopey expressions.

Kate Didn't you see she was upset?

Eddie Yeah.

Diannah Do you laugh everytime someone cries?

Eddie No.

Diannah When don't you laugh when someone cries?

Eddie When I find it not funny.

Diannah Can't you explain what was so hilarious just then?

Eddie No. Maybe you're a born comedian.

Kate (*Right into his face*) You haven't got any feelings at all, have you?

Eddie That's what you think. If you want me to go round with a straight face the whole time, I will. Or do you want me to be me?

Diannah Just try to understand people.

Eddie I understand and I laugh.

Diannah Eddie!! (*She calls out his name almost as though in*

panic. The urgency freezes everyone. They look at her. She is very emotional.)
It's not your laughing, it's that you never want to understand people. You never want to think of anybody else. What's so funny about me wanting my mum? What's so funny about that? Oh, I forgot, you're alright you've got a mum to nag away at you. You can say – 'oh shut up, mum, give it a rest . . .' I can't. I want to be able to but I can't and I feel like nothing, because I keep thinking 'what's wrong with me, what's the matter with me, to make my own mum not want me. What have I done? What could I possibly have done for my mum not to want me? She's chosen her boyfriend instead of me. I want my mum!' That's what you're laughing at! So why don't you just try to give other people's feelings some consideration. And at this moment I want you to give some consideration to mine.

(*Pause.*)

Linda What can he do Diannah? Diannah, what do you want him to do?

Ideas for development

1 Diannah says, 'I want my mum!'
Write down some of the circumstances in which you feel or have felt that you really need your parents. Compare with others. Have you come up with similar situations?
(i) Choose one of these situations and make up a scene to show how you feel and ask advice from parents and friends.
(ii) What is a situation where the last people you would wish to know about it are your parents?
(iii) Do you think some people sometimes take their parents for granted? Try a scene where you can see this.

2 Kate says, 'everyone has problems'. And everyone tends to feel that their problems are bigger than anyone else's. Create a situation in which one person's problems clash with the problems another person has.

3 Diannah says to Eddie, 'Just try and understand people'.
Do you think, like her, that Eddie is unsympathetic and unkind?
Eddie says to Diannah, 'I understand and I laugh'.
Do you think, like Eddie, that Eddie is the only realistic one?
How much can we 'really *do*' for each other?

4 Eddie sets himself up as the joker, always seeing the funny side of everything. Make up another scene in which someone is laughing at what is very serious for someone else.

5 A lot of comedy is made from laughter at someone else's misfortune e.g. a man slipping on a banana skin.
(i) Make up a little sequence to mime which might have come from a silent slap-stick movie.
(ii) Invent a situation which laughs at someone else's discomfort.
What is it about all this that makes for laughter?

6 Set up a scene where a group of friends at a party search the host's kitchen for food. Can the scene include several different attitudes to doing this?

7 Try some scenes in which two people meet at a party.

A Birthday

Joyce **John**
Eliza **Frances**

Late in the evening. They have just been refused entry to a club. They are falling about with laughter.

Joyce (*through her laughter*) I don't know whether I'm sixteen or eighteen.

Frances (*not believing what she has heard and laughing all the more*) What? What did you say? Say that again.

Joyce (*trying to be serious*) I don't know whether I'm sixteen or eighteen, okay.

Frances Excuse me Joyce, what are talking about?

Eliza What do you mean, you don't know how old you are?

John (*he's not laughing*) Don't talk rubbish Joyce. You got us thrown out . . . ruined the whole evening.

Joyce Look, for heaven's sake. I didn't know what to say, so I told the truth! I don't know whether I'm sixteen or eighteen years old . . . and that's just not a lot of fun. (*The others burst into laughter.*)

Eliza Oh, I know what she means. I could be seventeen or I could be – um – fifty-nine.

Frances Say it again, Joyce.

Joyce I could be sixteen or eighteen. (*Giggles again.*) I'm adopted.

Frances I know. So what?

John Joyce, just because you're adopted doesn't mean you're born twice. It only means you don't live with your real parents.

Joyce I've got two birthdays, right . . .
(*Roars of laughter.*)

Frances Two ages, two birthdays! Four parents!!

Joyce I give up on you lot. I'm trying to explain.

Eliza Sorry, Joyce, tell us then.

Joyce Well. listen. When I was born . . .

John Was this the first time or the action replay?

Joyce Hush up! I went to an orphanage and my parents

adopted me from there.

Frances And how old were you when your parents adopted you?

Joyce I don't know. (*The others laugh.*) I think I was either three or five..

Frances You don't know how old you were then, you don't know how old you are now. You don't sound all that organised to me.

(**John, Frances** *and* **Eliza** *find everything* **Joyce** *says funny.*)

Joyce The day I was adopted, that is my birthday as far as my parents are concerned.

Frances Which is what?

Joyce The seventeenth of July.

John Are you sure? (*He laughs.*)

Joyce But the day I arrived at the orphanage is the day they put down for my birthday, which is July the fifth.

Frances Which means that neither of them is the day you were actually born on. So you've got three birthdays!!

(*Howls of laughter.*)

Joyce Please.

Eliza Well, who put you in the orphanage? I mean whoever it was surely they must have said, 'Here's this kid, I can't look after her. She's such and such an age.'

(**Eliza** *makes a graphic gesture of handing the baby away as she speaks.*)

Joyce (*she is finding it less funny*) I don't know who brought me to the orphanage.

Frances I'm glad we didn't get into that club. This is much more fun.

Joyce When my parents got me from the orphanage, they didn't believe the age they'd given me. So they gave me another one.

Frances So you could have three ages. The one from your parents, the one from the orphanage and your real age. That would have confused the bouncer. 'How old are you, girly?'

'Sixteen, seventeen and eighteen.'

John And all stations to Southend. (*They laugh.*)

Eliza Why are you called Joyce?

Joyce That's the name my adopted parents gave me.

Frances You mean Joyce isn't your real name! How many names have you got?

John You could have three names.

Frances Three lots of birthday presents!

John But she wouldn't know who they were for. 'To Susan – here you are Samantha. It's another one for you.'

(*He acts out handing out presents, while the others laugh.*)

Eliza Why don't you go back to the orphanage and ask to look at your birth certificate?

Joyce I haven't got a birth certificate.

John Maybe, you weren't *born* at all.

Frances Go back to the orphanage and find out everything.

Joyce I don't want to. I'm afraid I might find out about my mum.

Frances Well, don't you want to? I would.

Joyce I've got a family now.

Eliza Go back and ask them . . .

John (*interrupting. He acts like a cowboy, smashing through saloon doors for a showdown.*) Boom! 'Give me my age!'

Joyce (*quietly, under the laughter of the others*) Shut up. Shut up. It just isn't funny any more.

Eliza If the orphanage don't know, how could you find out about your mum?

Joyce I've got a brother.

John Only one?

Eliza And how old might he be?

Frances Is he your real brother?

Joyce Yes.

Frances How do you know?

Joyce My adopted mum found that out.

Frances Well, then your adopted mum must know who your real mum is.

Eliza And your real age.

John And your real name.

Joyce Yes, but . . . no, but . . . oh, go away, leave me alone.

(*They see Joyce is upset.*)

Frances Oh, look, I'm sorry Joyce.

Eliza Joyce!? You're probably not even called Joyce.

Frances Yes, that's right. From now on, I'm going to call you Constance!

John Don't be wicked. (*They laugh.*)

Eliza No, not Constance . . . Marion!

Frances No, I'm going to call you Constance. Hallo Constance.

(**Frances** *goes up to* **Joyce** *as if to shake hands with her.* **Joyce** *runs away.*)

Ideas for development

1 Joyce says she does not want to find out about her natural mother. If you were adopted, would you want to find out?
(i) Assume you are adopted and you have found out your natural mother's address. Write her a letter.
(ii) Write a letter to a close friend about your feelings on discovering you are adopted.

2 (i) Plan a scene in which everybody sends one character to coventry.
(ii) After that scene is shown, ask that character to describe how he or she felt during the scene.

3 Prepare a scene in which several people are hurting the feelings of someone in their group, but they are unaware of what they are doing.

4 (i) Write a description of yourself which is made up of actual 'facts'. Your age, your hair colour, family, etc.
(ii) Write a description of yourself which includes no 'facts', only the feelings and attitudes you have.

5 Do you think it makes any difference whether you are adopted or brought up by your real parents?

Richard on the Floor

Richard **Gary** **Tim**
Lorna **Kelvin**

In a common room. We are watching this particular group. However, there may be other groups in the common room, each involved in their own discussions. The publicness of the place makes **Richard** *particularly vulnerable. He is sitting on a chair, looking very miserable.* **Gary** *stands over him.* **Lorna** *and* **Tim** *watch from a distance, only partly drawn into the scene by a casual interest. They are eating.* **Tim** *does not speak but his expression always makes it quite clear whose side he is on.*

Gary I don't know why you take it, Richard.

Richard Shut up, alright, just shut up!

Gary I wouldn't take it. You shouldn't get pushed around like you do!

Richard I don't get pushed around.

Gary You do, Richard, you do.

Richard I don't get pushed around.

Lorna Yes, you do.

Gary Always, trying to be the nice guy!

Richard Leave me alone. I don't want to talk about it.

Gary You should try being selfish for once, Richard.

Richard Like you?

Gary Yeah, like me.

Lorna Yeah, it works – look at Gary.

Richard Yeah, look at Gary.

Lorna He's successful – it works.

Gary (*to* **Lorna**) Have you ever seen me in a state like that? (*He points at* **Richard**.)

Richard You don't know what it's about.

Gary I do. This woman! If this woman had said 'Oh look, there's a fish playing football', You'd have gone, 'Oh yeah, a fish playing football. (**Tim** *laughs.*)

Richard You don't understand.

Gary And just what is there to understand? She orders you about like . . . like she's a bloke!

Richard She doesn't order me about.

Lorna Yes, she does.

Gary She's got you well under control. Did whatever she wanted.
Richard No, I did what I wanted.
Gary Sure. It just happened to be the things she wanted.
Richard So?
Gary So, she gets her way all the time.
Richard No. (*Pause.*) She got her way sometimes, yeah.
Lorna Most of the time!
Gary All of the time!
Richard Not all of the time.
Gary You ought to take a leaf out of her book and be tougher.
Richard You ought to take a leaf out of her book and sod off.
Gary She's left you now, hasn't she? So what are you going to do about it?
Richard I'm not going to do anything about it. I'm going to sit here and feel sorry for myself, okay?
Lorna Oh, Gary, leave him.
Richard Shut up, Lorna. I don't see what it's got to do with you.
Gary It's got a lot to do with us.
Richard It's got nothing to do with you.
Gary I don't know what's the matter with you sometimes. You ask for it, if you ask me.
Richard How do I ask for it?
Lorna Being soppy.
Richard Soppy! Soppy! Oh great, my friends. I come to them in need and they tell me I'm soppy.
Gary The girl's a bitch, anyway.
Richard She wasn't a bitch.
Lorna She wasn't a bitch . . . but . . .
Gary She was a bitch. I saw the power play she was pulling.
Richard Shut up, Gary.
Gary I'm going to speak my mind.
Richard No, you're not, because I'm going to stop you.
Gary Oh yes – and how are you going to stop me?
Lorna Calm down, right, calm down.
Gary Well, some of the things she did! She gave Richard a comb and says, 'Richard, comb your hair'. And the idiot combs his hair because some woman tells him.
Richard Gary, shut up.
(**Richard** *hits out at* **Gary**.)
Gary Don't push me, Richard.

Richard Why not? It's okay for you to pull me apart but I'm not allowed to touch you?

Gary You're getting violent, Rich, that's unlike you. See what the girl did to you, stupid bitch.

Richard Gary!

Gary Well, she is a bitch, look what she's done to you.

Richard Gary, don't make me fight you.

Gary What? I'm doing this for your own good.

Richard What have I done to you?

Gary You haven't done anything to me.

Richard Well, get off my back and leave me alone then.

Gary You're a friend aren't you. Well, I'm trying to help you, aren't I?

Richard I don't want you to help me. I don't want you to do anything, just leave me alone!

(**Richard** *pushes* **Gary** *again.* **Gary** *tightens and squares up to* **Richard**.)

Gary Don't do that again, Richard, I mean it.

Richard What's it got to do with you.

Lorna Calm down.

Richard Keep out of it, Lorna. What's it got to do with any of you?

Lorna Carry on then. Beat each others brains out. I don't care.

Gary (*he is relaxed again*) Serves you right for going out with feminists, anyway.

Richard Is that what you put it down to?

Gary Yeah!

Richard (*He stares at* **Gary**. *He cannot believe this last statement.*)
I don't believe you.

(*Silence.*)

Gary (**Gary** *is ridiculing* **Richard**. *He mimics how* **Richard** *behaves when he is with his girlfriend.*)
'Is my hair straight? Should it be a bit more over to this side?

Richard Shut up!

(**Richard** *suddenly flies at* **Gary**. *They crash to the floor as they fight.* **Gary** *easily pins* **Richard** *to the floor and* *holds him there so he is unable to move.*)

Gary Behave Richard, behave! (*He is holding him still. Then he quickly gets up and moves far away.* **Richard** *stays on the floor defeated.*)
I'm sorry Rich. (*Pause.*) Well, what more do you want me to say. I've said I'm sorry.

(*Silence.*)

Lorna Richard, get up off the floor.
Gary Come on, Richard. It doesn't become you to sulk.
Lorna Richard, get up.

(**Kelvin** *a mate of* **Gary's** *enters the scene. He is sharp enough to take* **Gary** *on. He has an air of authority. As he meets them all, he begins to understand what is happening and can look at it more cooly than the others.*)

Kelvin Richard. Gary. Others – hi.
Gary Alright, Kelvin? Richard, get up.
Kelvin Alright, Richard? (**Kelvin** *goes up to* **Richard** *and slaps him on the back.* **Gary** *rounds on him.*)
Gary Leave him alone.
Kelvin Are you telling me to leave him alone?
Gary Stop patronising him! That's the trouble with all you people, you patronise.
Lorna Leave him alone.
Gary And you shut up.
Lorna I haven't done anything, either.
Gary It's you people who make him the way he is.
Kelvin What do you mean 'you people'? Hang about, who are you pointing accusations at – bastard?
Gary Don't call me a bastard.
Kelvin I'll call you what I like.
Gary (*His tone changes as he tries to pacify* **Kelvin**.)
Look, don't be silly, I don't want to fight with you.
Kelvin And I don't want to fight with you. Tell me what's happening.
Gary I don't want to talk about it.
Kelvin Don't be daft. What do you mean, you don't want to talk about it? You start flinging accusations around and then you say you don't want to talk about it. What's the matter with you? We're supposed to be friends.

Gary Yes, we are.
Kelvin Well, what's all this abuse of my other friends then?
Gary I was only trying to help.
Kelvin Is that what you call it?
Gary You're just patronising.
Kelvin Am I?
Gary As per usual.
Kelvin What do you mean, 'as per usual'? I'm trying to help. Why are you so violent, Gary? I bet it was over his bird, ay? At least the guy's got a bird.
Gary That's the whole point.
Kelvin Well, what's going on then? Educate me.
Gary He got this bird – and the bird pecked him!
Kelvin Funny that!
Gary It's not supposed to be funny.
Kelvin You're always taking advantage of Richard. Just go easy on him.
Gary I am easy on him.
Kelvin You're always embarrassing him.
Gary He embarrasses himself. Look at the guy.
(*He points at* **Richard** *on the floor. They all look at him.*)
Kelvin Apologise.
Gary I have apologised.
Kelvin Pick the bloke up.
Gary Eh?
Kelvin Pick him up! What's he sitting on the floor for?
Gary I don't know why he's sitting on the floor. It's not like him to just sit on the floor . . . and shut up.
Lorna He's sulking.
Kelvin Because of what you've done, Gary, right? Loopy you are. Mental.

(**Kelvin** *goes across to* **Richard**.)

Richard, don't be a baby. Get up.
(*He goes very close to* **Richard** *and bends down so their faces are almost touching.*)
Richard Leave me alone.
Kelvin No, I won't leave you alone. You can spend the rest of your life being left alone. And where will that get you? It'll get you nowhere – apart from a life of sitting on the floor crying. And that doesn't amount to an awful lot, does it. See? I'm your friend. I'm thinking of you, so I won't leave you alone.

Lorna (*from some distance away*) Haven't you two done enough damage already?

Richard (*to* **Kelvin**. *Their conversation is quiet and private*) Look, sometimes I feel I don't want to talk to anyone about anything. So I don't want to tell you, Kelvin, all about it. And I don't want to tell Gary all about it. I just want to be left alone.

Kelvin Well then, don't tell me all about it. Why didn't you tell Gary to keep his snout out?

Richard I did but he wouldn't listen. He just kept on and on.

Lorna There you are – you let yourself be pushed around.

Gary (**Gary** *calls to* **Richard** *from a way away*) Richard, get up!

Kelvin (**Kelvin** *is still close to* **Richard** *and continues to whisper to him.*) On your feet, Richard.

Gary Richard, get up.

Kelvin Hey, Richard?

Richard What?

Kelvin Come on.

Richard Kelvin.

Kelvin Snap out of it.

Richard I'm cool.

Kelvin You're tense, Rich, come on.

Richard I'm okay.

Kelvin You're losing to him, Rich.

Richard I don't have to be like Gary.

Kelvin You've got to be able to take him on, though. (**Gary** *comes up behind* **Richard** *and pulls him to his feet.*)

Gary Come on, mate. Let's go for a drink.

Richard I don't like you much right now, Gary.

Gary No, of course, you don't at the moment. But you will, Richard you will. Later you and I will be mates again, won't we. So why don't we forget all about this and be friends. It's like when you're a kid and you fall into the snow. You're cold and miserable but you know really soon you're going to be warm and indoors.

Richard Yes. I'm sorry mate.

Kelvin Wait a minute. What are you apologising to him for?

Richard Because he's my mate, Kelvin.

Gary Let's have a drink.

Richard Yeah.

Gary Got any money?

Richard Yeah.

(*They go off.*)

Kelvin I don't believe those two. I just don't believe it.

(*He goes.*)

Lorna Exciting, wasn't it?

(*She goes.*)

Tim (*still eating*) Ummm.

Ideas for development

1 (i) Set up a scene showing Richard and his girlfriend together the day before this incident took place.
(ii) Set up a scene showing Richard and his girlfriend together the day after this incident takes place.

2 Suppose Richard's girlfriend hears about this incident. How do you think she would feel? What do you think would happen if she confronted Gary about his interference? Show this confrontation.

3 Is Richard being 'soppy'?

4 Gary says, 'Later you and I will be mates again, won't we?' How far can friendship be pushed? Set out a scene where a close friendship is put to the test.

5 This scene happens in a common room.
(i) Try setting up the other activities in the common room.
(ii) Work out another incident which might break out in a common room.
(iii) How does it affect Richard that this scene happens in a public place? Create a scene in which someone is embarrassed partly because something they feel is private is happenning in public.

6 Gary says, 'She orders you about like she was a bloke.' What does he mean? What effects do comments like these have on women?

7 Gary seems to think that you must be tough to survive. Kelvin seems to disagree with him about how to be tough, yet he says to Richard, 'you've got to be able to take the guy on'. Discuss their attitudes to standing up for oneself. Work out another situation where standing up for yourself is all-important.

Natalie Wood

Carlton **Carole**

Paul

Watching television at **Paul's** *house.* **Carlton** *is in a bad mood. Everything that the others say makes him feel more alone and angry. He himself, really wants to say nothing. The quarrel seems ridiculous. The lines go very fast, like a squabble about nothing. They almost sound like small children. But soon it is not just about the television and it becomes more personally spiteful.*

Carlton Isn't that Natalie Wood?
Carole Elizabeth Taylor.

(*Pause.*)

Carlton Natalie Wood.
Carole Elizabeth Taylor!
Carlton I never forget a face.
Carole Well, you've forgotten that one. That's Elizabeth Taylor. She stars in *National Velvet*.
Carlton Natalie Wood stars in *National Velvet*.
Carole No. She was in *Rebel Without a Cause*. This is *National Velvet* and that is Elizabeth Taylor.
Carlton Don't be stupid.
Carole I'm not being stupid. You're being stupid.
Paul It is Carlton.
Carole Yes! Isn't it!
Paul This is Elizabeth Taylor.
Carole You're always getting things wrong and pretending you haven't.
Carlton Not!
Carole Are!
(*There is a sulky pause, while they watch TV.*)
You started it. You're always doing this.
Paul Natalie Wood! (*He roars with laughter.*)
Carlton Alright! Alright!
Carole (*to* **Paul**) Listen. I say the pub we usually go to is called 'The Castle'. Mr. Big, here, reckons it's called 'The Bird in the Hand'. He refuses to back down. Even when he asked the flaming landlord.
Carlton Pardon?
Carole You heard.

Paul Here, look Carlton. There's Dick van Dyke.
Carlton Okay, Paul.
Carole All I want you to do is say 'I am wrong'.
Carlton To you . . . no, never, no way, ever, shut up.
Paul You'll never get that guy to admit that, never.
Carlton (*trying to shut off from the argument*) Do you want to watch the film or what?
Carole (*pointing at the TV*) Oh look, she's going to fall. (*disappointed*) Oh, she didn't.
Paul I've seen this before. It's boring anyway.
Carole Who did it have in it last time?
(**Paul** *laughs again.*)
Carlton Alright, that's enough you two.
Carole Oh, Sir! (*Salutes at* **Carlton**.)
Paul (*taking the mickey*) That's a good imitation of Tommy Cooper.

(**Carlton** *stands up, angrily.*)

Paul What's the matter with you, Carlton?
Carole You're never usually like this.
Carlton Mind your own business. Just forget it.
Paul It was only a joke, man.
Carlton Well, just shut up will you – 'man'.
Paul He's upset. (*He finds it funny.*)
Carlton (*pointing at* **Paul's** *mouth*) You see those two rubber things there, well just shut them. I want to watch the film, so shut up.
Paul Don't tell me to shut up.
Carlton And what are you going to do about it?
Paul Eh! Are you challenging me now Carlton?
Carlton Paul, just rest now.
Paul Who are you telling to rest now Carlton?
Carlton You, right.
(**Carlton** *pushes* **Paul**. **Paul** *pushes back. Quickly they are on the floor wrestling.*)
Carole (*she is trying to pull them apart*) Stop it! Idiots! Barbarian! (**Paul** *and* **Carlton** *separate*) I thought you'd broken your neck Paul.
Carlton Pity, isn't it. (*He kicks out at* **Paul** *in a half-hearted way as the tension winds down. They settle.*)
Paul What's the matter with you? I've never seen you like this. What's happened to the mild mannered gentleman? All because of a film starring Elizabeth Taylor.

Carole You two are like a couple of housewives. (**Paul** *sees the funny side of it and begins to giggle.*) And you stop laughing.

Paul Well, I've never seen him like this. (*Pause.*) What's happening Carlton?

(**Carole** *takes the television and pulls it towards her. She lies on her stomach, with her face close to the screen, blocking the others out.* **Paul** *has been watching* **Carlton**.)

Carlton Drop it okay. (*He is quiet.*)

Paul (*matching* **Carlton's** *mood*) Don't talk to me like that. That wasn't you. I know you.

Carlton Well, you don't know me well enough.

(*They are not arguing. In the calm after the storm they really want to understand.*)

Paul Carlton, don't say that I don't know you.

Carlton I didn't say that.

Paul I know you.

Carlton You just said you have never seen me like that.

Paul It's not like you to be violent, no.

Carlton Perhaps you just don't know that side of me.

Paul Carlton, you're my friend.

Carlton Oh yeah, and what's a friend? Who are my friends?

Paul Friends, you know, friends.

(*Pause.*)

My mum always used to say to me 'make sure as you go through life, at a time of a crisis, you can call out and there'll be someone there to help you'. A friend, Carlton. She drilled that into me.

(*Silence.*)

Carlton Have you got any friends?

Paul Yeah.

Carlton I mean, real friends.

Paul Yeah.

Carlton How many?

Paul About five. Yeah five.

Carlton I don't believe you.

Paul Five real friends. I'm including you in that.

Carlton Five? Not your Christmas card list. Real friends.

Paul I said – I'm including you in that five.

Carlton Five. Well, you're lucky, because most people can only count two at the most.

Paul (*He is disturbed by* **Carlton's** *lack of response to him.*) If I asked you how many friends you'd got, would I be in your number? I wouldn't be, would I? (*Pause.*) You'd say, 'I don't have any friends' wouldn't you?

Carlton If you were a friend you'd understand what I'm asking now.

Paul You haven't answered my question, Carlton.

Carlton What do you want me to say?

Paul Truth.

Carlton You're my partner (*He sends up the idea a little, making 'partner' sound jokily sinister.*)

Paul Truth?

Carlton Yeah.

Ideas for development

1 Why is it that sometimes you can take a joke and other times not? Do you think Carlton is justified in getting upset?

2 (i) Plan a scene entitled 'The Argument'.
   (ii) Look at how the argument in the scene you planned started. Discuss whether you think arguments are sparked off by little things or major events.
3 Invent a scene where someone has come home feeling miserable and depressed and mopes about while normal home life goes on around. Allow an opportunity for this character to explain his or her feelings.
4 Do you think that real friends argue? If so, why?
   (i) Prepare a scene in which friends have a quarrel, which they know is not going to affect their friendship.
   (ii) Prepare another scene where the disagreement between the friends may well affect their friendship.
5 Suppose that after the film Carlton, Carole and Paul go for a drink at 'The Castle'. Show what may happen in the pub.
6 Write down for yourself your answer to Paul's question: 'Have you got any friends . . . I mean real friends?'
Carry on to say what the difference is between friends and real friends.
7 In an argument, do you think that violence ever achieves anything?

Can you Hear Me?

Mick **Tony**

In this scene the actions are as important as the words. **Mick's** *silence is essential to the atmosphere created.*

Mick *sits alone, chewing gum.* **Tony** *walks by, sees him and from a distance shouts out his name.*

Tony Mick!

(**Mick** *makes no response.* **Tony** *walks up to him. For a moment* **Mick** *stops chewing.*)

Tony Where the hell were you last night? You promised you'd come with me and then you just didn't bother to turn up. What was the matter?

(**Mick** *glances at* **Tony**, *but still does not answer. His silence is threatening.*)

Tony Were you in your bed, ay? Hiding under your covers? Can't you think of nothing to say to me now? Too ashamed to say something? Because you're a coward!

(**Mick** *looks at him.*)

Tony I've hit the nail on the head, haven't I? I should have realized just what you were. A coward. You make me sick. I thought I trusted you. No. I was an idiot. Last night you let me down.

(**Tony** *is getting frantic for a reaction.*)

Tony What did you do it to me for? (*desparately*) Ay? Why do you put on this act the whole time? Why don't you just say what goes on in your yellow head? (**Tony** *is in the swing of it now, seeing how far he can push* **Mick**.) When it comes down to it, you're nothing. Nothing. I don't even like looking at you now. You remind me of something I step in on a hot day. I'd better stand down wind of you.

(**Mick** *stares him out.*)

Tony Don't look at me, Mick. I trusted you. Why don't you say something.

(**Tony** *gives up and walks away, fed up. He stands some way away staring at* **Mick**.)

Tony (*Almost talking to himself.*)
Mick you must have some answer in your head you'd like to tell me. Mick!

(**Tony** *goes back up to* **Mick**, *in a fury.)*

Tony Look, Just explain why you didn't turn up, okay? Maybe you're not a coward. (*yelling*) Say something! You . . . I'll kick your head in.

(**Tony** *kicks* **Mick**. **Mick** *stiffens but sits motionless. Pause.* **Tony** *kicks him again.*)

Tony What would you do if I keep on kicking you, then? Say something.

(**Mick** *takes a packet of chewing gum out of his pocket and holds a stick out to him.* **Tony** *hits it out of his hand.* **Mick** *holds out another stick.* **Tony** *hits that out of his hand.*)

Tony Get off with your sweets. Jesus. You're driving me crazy.

(*Silence.* **Tony** *goes up really close to* **Mick's** *ear.*)

Tony What's holding you back? Come on, Mick. I bet you're really listening to me. I bet you're really having a struggle to keep those lips closed. Why don't you say what you're feeling instead of holding it all inside, making you feel ill.

(*Suddenly,* **Mick** *stands up and squares up to* **Tony**.)

Tony Oh, yeah. And what are you going to do now? Hit me with your handbag? Spit Chanel No. 5 in my face?

(**Mick**, *stony faced, moves to sit down.* **Tony** *moves very fast and kicks the chair from under him.* **Mick** *lands on the floor. Immediately he stands up, faces* **Tony**.)

Tony Look, I'm sorry, okay Mick! I'm sorry. We've been friends for a long time now. What have I done to you? I haven't done anything. (*Pause*) So what's all this silence act?

(**Mick** *turns his back on* **Tony**, *to pick up his chair.*)

Tony I'm talking to you Mick. Oh, forget it.
(**Mick** *has sat down again and is opening up a new piece of gum.*)
Don't let our friendship break up now. All you have to do is say a few little words about why you weren't there. Look, I don't believe you backed out, okay. But look at it from my point of view.

Ideas for development

1 What thoughts are going through Mick's head during the scene? Try writing them down to form a monologue.

2 Work in pairs for this exercise.
One person sits on a chair, determined not to communicate in any way. The other person attempts to get his or her partner to communicate. (No physical contact is allowed.)
The rest of the group can sit in a circle around the action, trying to spot any sign of communication, for example, a person laughing or making a gesture is communication as much as speech.

3 (i) Again, watch the action in a circle.
One person sits on a chair in the middle. Another enters the circle and begins a scene, with the line:
'Where the hell were you last night?'
There should be no time for planning.

(ii) After the scene has got going, try adding an extra person from the circle.
The newcomer should take one person's side.
See how many people you can add to the scene and still keep it going.

The Promotion

Rob **Tom**

In a G.P.O. sorting office. **Tom** *and* **Rob** *are placing letters into pigeon holes.*

Rob I got the promotion.
Tom Oh yeah? Postmaster?
Rob Look Tom, I've been meaning to tell you.
Tom Oh yeah? Don't talk rubbish.
Rob You know old Mooney has left . . .
Tom Yeah.
Rob . . . I got his job. Sorting supervisor.

(*Pause.* **Tom** *stops work and looks at* **Rob**.)

Tom What do you mean sorting supervisor?
Rob Supervisor.
Tom So how did you get a supervisor's job? How did you get it?
Rob They came and asked me today. This afternoon.
Tom They came and asked you? You?
Rob Yeah.
Tom They asked you?
Rob Yeah.
Tom They didn't ask me, they asked you?
Rob Yeah. What's the matter?
Tom You're joking, aren't you?
Rob I'm not joking. You want to see the slip?
Tom I don't want to see the slip. (*Pause.*) I just don't see why you should get it and not anybody else.
Rob Why not?
Tom Well, I've been here longer than you.
Rob You muck about all the time.
Tom What do you mean 'muck about'?
Rob Well, come on Tom, you don't do anything.
Tom Well, you don't do anything.
Rob Look, I do more than you do.
Tom Rubbish! I've been doing this job longer than you and you get the supervisor's job.

(*They carry on sorting the letters in silence.*)

Rob Does it really matter?
Tom They couldn't even get a uniform your size and you come in and get supervisor.
Rob They'll get one now, don't worry about that. And I won't be at the bus stop tomorrow, because I start at ten, not nine.
(**Tom** *stares at* **Rob**.)
And I finish at four, not six. And I don't work Sundays.
(*Pause.*)
I didn't want to tell you, you know. I didn't want to get you angry. But now I don't give a damm – now I'm glad. Now I'm glad. I'm one level higher than you. I bet it's you who feels small now, isn't it?
Tom I don't feel small.
Rob Now who's uniform won't fit, eh? Mine fits me now.
Tom You're the luckiest git I know.
Rob Hard work.
Tom Hard work, my ass! You do sod all!
Rob Well, I do sod all a bit better than you do!

(*Pause. They continue sorting.*)

Tom Sorting supervisor, huh?
Rob And when you're on the line and you do something wrong, I'm going to come down on you like a ton of bricks.
Tom Yeah? It'll be the last thing you do.
Rob You'll be surprised, mate.
Tom And you'll be surprised as well.
Rob You've got a sore head, Tom, that's your problem.
Tom And you'll have no head in a minute – big as it is.
Rob It is big, because it's got something to be big about. I'm one up on you. I'm one of them now, with the silver badges I'll get for my lapels.
Tom Well listen, don't come round giving me any of your 'do this' rubbish, all this governors talk, because I won't listen to you. You know nothing about sorting, anyway.

(*Pause.*)

Rob I might get a car with my extra money.

Tom When do you start?
Rob Monday.
Tom Monday?
Rob So I won't be coming into work on Sunday.
Tom You don't need the overtime now, I suppose?
Rob No.
Tom I won't be seeing you down the bus stop, then?
Rob No.
Tom I just hope you don't get any funny ideas, alright . . . coming round in your fancy gear telling me to do this and that.

(*Pause.* **Rob** *makes a gesture to try and repair the relationship.*)

Rob Does it matter? I mean, just because I'm higher than you at work . . . Can't we be the same outside?
Tom So you won't be going to the bus stop anymore? You won't be doing any of the things we used to do? (*He continues to work in silence.*)

Ideas for development

1 (i) Show the scene of Tom and Rob at the bus stop, the morning before they hear the news of Rob's promotion.
(ii) Show them at the bus stop again a week later, with Rob in his new job.

2 Prepare a scene in which someone is suddenly 'bigger' than his or her friends for some reason other than promotion. Consider the different reactions which others may have. Will that character act 'big' or try to hide it? Will friends welcome or resist the change?

3 Suppose Tom rather than Rob had got the promotion. Show a scene where Tom breaks the news to Rob.

4 Imagine yourself to be working.

(i) Write a letter to your boss asking for promotion, stating why you think you deserve it.

(ii) See if the class or group you are in can make a selection from these applications and decide to whom they would give promotion.

Monologues

A Postman

Mick *is talking about his job, as if across the table in a pub with a friend.*

When I walk down the street, I get respect. People respect a uniform.

I was down the tube the other day, the doors had just shut – but the guard opened them up for me. He saw the uniform, you see, and saw who I was. He knew I was with the GPO. People respect that you're doing something.

Like the other day, I was walking down the road, right, and there were these two coppers walking towards me. They parted – and I walked between them. If I'd have had my ordinary clothes on, my flight jacket or something, I'd have had to move. But with the uniform they could see I was someone, and they gave me a bit of respect. It's something, you see.

No, it's alright really, with the GPO. I have money in my pocket – enough to treat my mum to a little something at the end of the week and have a drink or buy a jumper, you know. Of course, when you're on 'lates' you might get a bit fed up, but, you know, you stick with the GPO you can do plenty of things. I mean, you can drive if you like that, or you can deliver or you can go for your PHG: Postman Higher Grade. See and again, people respect you for that, because they can see you've done something. Yeah – respect.

Nice little pension, and all. So if you wanted to stop with the GPO the sky's the limit, like.

I used to work in a timber yard. I was coming home on the bus all covered in sawdust. I felt really dirty. Had to have a bath before I could even to out for a drink. I thought to myself, there's got to be more than a timber yard. So, now I've got this.

Let's face it, there's millions of people out there called Mick . . . but I know which one I am.

9.38

David, *alone in his flat.*

Here I am – talking to myself – again!!

9.38.

Before I got a flat and started living on my own, it was always about twenty to ten. Now, it's 9.38.

Perhaps I should jam the clock, so that it jumps from 9.37 to 9.39. Then there wouldn't be a 9.38. But then I suppose it would be like hospital. Because they don't have a bed 13 in hospital, do they, because the people who get bed 13 think they're going to die. So they go from bed 12 to bed 14, but the only trouble is, the poor sods in bed 12 and 14 both think they've got bed 13. Well, it would be the same, wouldn't it? If you tried to pretend that 9.38 just doesn't exist.

At about 9.30 I start the washing up, hoping that by 9.38 I'll be so engrossed in the dishes that I'll forget all about 9.38 . . . It never happens though. I spend the whole time thinking – 'can't be far off 9.38 right now'.

(*Pause.* **David** *is mouching about the flat, trying to distract himself.*)

What did I do last 9.38? Thought about 9.38, I suppose.

Perhaps I should put a record on. I mean, 9.38 is too early to go to bed and too late to start anything. I mean, if I started any work, I'd only have about half an hour then I'd want to go to bed.

I wonder if it's 9.38 all over the world?

It lasts so long as well. It lasts for ever.

The thing about a digital clock is everything is so precise. It wakes you up in the morning at 7.45 – exactly. I mean, my old alarm used to go off at any old time.

(*His nose is pressed against the window. He speaks slowly and mysteriously, as though telling a ghost story.*)

I can imagine thousands and thousands of people, up and down the country all sitting behind their windows . . . waiting . . . for 9.38.

(*Snapping out of it.*)

I think I'll put a record on, now. Yeah! That's what I'll do. I'll put a record on. Wow!

(*He claps his hands together as if really excited. He is encouraging himself.*)

Michael's World

Michael *is alone in his room, playing with a hat and cane, posing. He catches sight of himself in the mirror. He walks up to talk to the person he sees reflected there.*

Hallo. Um, I'm sorry, I can't quite place you. What line of business are you in? Oh yeah? Oh, I know who you are . . . you're me. Ah.

What's it like in that mirror. It's bloody horrible out here. I've always wanted to get into a mirror. Where have you been?

(*He is listening for an answer. The character in the mirror has been into space.*)

Oh! I've always wanted to go into space, you know. Have you been to Mars and Jupiter and that lot? . . . You have!! Tell me, have they got life on them? . . . Oh go on, you can tell me. Oh come on. I'll give you a pound if you do . . .

. . . You've been to Graption? Where's Graption? I've never heard of it. Well, what kind of life have they got there then? . . . The same as us. It can't be that bad surely.

(*He steps back. He might leave the character in the mirror. He decides not to.*)

How long are you going to stay in there?

(*Mock horror. The character has insulted him.*)

What do you mean, you don't like my manners. I don't like them myself. (*He becomes a tough thirties gangster with an american accent. Fast, cool talking*) I grieve over them, long winter evenings, I don't mind you ritzing me or drinking lunch out of a bottle, but don't waste your time trying to cross examine me, okay?

(*A sudden big grin*) Humphrey Bogart said that, you know. I've always wanted to say that to someone. You're the only one who would listen.

(*He stares at himself intensely, pulling faces.*)

Why are you staring at me? I don't like the look of you anymore. I'm going to hit you one of these days. (*A sudden new thought strikes him.*)

Hey! Have you met any famous people in there? Errol Flynn?! Yeah? . . . What's he like? Is he really good with a sword? Yeah? . . . And does he really . . . you know . . . well, I read in a book somewhere . . . Yeah?

Who else is in there, then? Gandhi? Well, isn't it peaceful in there? Are there wars in there as well? . . . Oh, that's bad. I mean, we have wars out here, but I didn't think you had wars in there.

(*He watches himself posing for a moment.*)

Why do you wear a hat? . . . Because I wear one? That's no reason. You shouldn't copy people, you know. Look I'll take mine off. (**Michael** *takes his hat off*) Hey! You keep yours on. You copy cat. (*He puts his hat back on*) You're doing it again. That's a nice cane. Hey! Are there any pretty girls in there? I'm always looking for pretty girls but . . . (*Back comes the american gangster*) . . . hell, I can't do nothing about it. Have you got any tips? Yeah? Well, here goes . . .

(*He throws himself into a dance routine, using the cane and the hat. He is being Fred Astaire. The character in the mirror is his audience. He stops. Eyes himself up. Squares up, narrows his eyes – the hard talking gangster . . .*)

Hallo again. I've come to talk to you serious. I don't wanna talk about your make-believe world anymore. I'm talking about what's out here. And what's out here is me, see? Not you. Me. Alright? I mean, who the hell are you? In fact, it's not who are you. It's who am I.

One in a Crowd

Jackie *tells this story, acting it out to make it more vivid.*

The other day, I went down to the station. It was absolutely packed. And I went into one of those photo booths. (*She goes through the actions as she speaks.*) I went in, sat down and put my money in. And then I noticed this pair of legs the other side of the curtain. I thought nothing of it.

I waited for the red pose sign to come up; it did and I posed – (*she poses each time*) – and again – and the last time. Then I came out of the photo booth . . . (*standing up*) . . . and this pair of legs is still there. It was this old lady. She was standing there staring at me. I smiled at her. She just stared. I thought, 'here we go'.

I said to her, 'are you waiting for your photos too?' She just stood there, staring.

Then she said, (**Jackie** *puts on the character of the old lady*) 'You don't look like other people, do you?'

I thought, 'not like other people? What do other people look like, then?' I said to her, 'I am, I'm just like other people'.

Then she said, (*as old lady*) 'Why do you dress the way you do? What's in your mind that you dress like that?'

'Everyone dresses like this,' I said. 'What does she mean, what does she mean,' I think. I was just wearing this gear. (*She indicates what she is wearing. It is not ordinary. Then, as the old lady . . .*)

'But you must think differently'?

(*as herself*) 'Differently? Differently from whom?'

The photos had come through by now. And I thought to myself, 'how can I explain to this person that underneath the tweed suit and the furry hat, we're pretty much the same'. So, I said to her, 'If I was wearing, what you're wearing, you wouldn't be asking me this question'. I thought 'I've got her, I've got her'. (*She turns as if to confront the old lady*) . . . But she'd gone.

This woman came out of nowhere – out of the crowd – noticed me – and was gone again.

Ideas for development

It is in the monologues that the central theme of *Get Out of That, Then!* are in some ways most clearly expressed. A person is talking about what sets him or her apart from the crowd which is everyone else. But at the same time, everyone in the crowd has a story that counts.

1 Write about yourself. What sets you apart?
What do you have to say for yourself?
Try reading outloud to others what you have written.

2 Write about yourself. Do you ever feel you are alone?
What would life be like with no-one caring about you?
Try reading that outloud too.

3 Take on a character. Say a few sentences that describe the character, a few facts. Let other people develop that character for you by asking questions: what do you do, like, think, your history, etc. Answer in character and see how much detail about that character you can create.

A Postman

Speak for approximately a minute on what you think gives you respect for yourself and leads others to respect you.

9.38

Create a scene where you are alone in your room talking to yourself.

Michael's World

(i) Sit in front of a mirror for a while and write down what you see. Maybe you can try reading it aloud. Or is it too personal?
Or

(ii) Do a short scene of someone alone in front of a mirror.

One in a Crowd

(i) Tell a story to everyone about something funny that happened to you.

(ii) Write or speak about a stranger you noticed in a crowd.

(iii) Do you feel you could be spotted in a crowd? Why?

Giselle's Diary

(This scene is a follow-on to 'The Diary' which begins *Get Out of That, Then!*)

Ben **Giselle** .

Ben, *a friend of* **Giselle's**, *has dropped by to visit and found her in her room, writing her diary.*

Ben (*friendly*) What are you doing?

Giselle (*She is slightly embarrassed that he has found her writing her diary and so closes it, but keeps the place with her finger.*)
It's only my diary.

Ben Oh, I'm sorry. I won't be nosey.

Giselle It's okay.

(*Pause. They both feel uneasy.*)

Ben So how's things.

Giselle Okay. And with you?

Ben Not too bad. Not too bad. Hey look, don't let me disturb you.

Giselle It's hard to write when someone comes, you know.

Ben Do you want me to go?

Giselle It's okay. I can always do it later on.

(*Pause.*)

Ben (*he grins suddenly*) Is there anything about me in there?

Giselle (*she thinks about the answer*) Yeah.

Ben (*cheekily*) Yeah? Will you show me? (*Pause.*)

Giselle (*she opens the diary and pushes it towards him*) There.

Ben Will you read it to me?

Giselle I couldn't do that. If you really want to know, you could read it.
(**Ben** *starts to read.*)
It's just what I thought but couldn't actually say.
(*Silence as* **Ben** *reads.*)

Ben Giselle . . . why don't you say these things?

Giselle I can't – because you don't let me.

Ben What do you mean, I don't let you. You just have to say it. You've shown me, so just say it.

Giselle Well, I don't always feel clear enough to say that sort of thing. I just feel it. That's why my diary matters, right, because that's where I can say it.

Ben (*He is obviously moved*) Thanks for letting me read it. (*Pause.*) I don't know what to say, really . . . I'd like to read more sometime.

Giselle Okay. (*She feels she can trust him further.*) Don't you ever feel that when you're in a group of people and they're all talking away . . . there are things in your head that you couldn't tell anyone . . . but you need to get them down – out of your system somehow?

Ben If I feel something is important enough to say to someone then I say it to them. And if I don't, I just don't. (*Pause.*) But, I understand you more now. Thank you.

Ideas for development

1 In this scene, Giselle makes a gesture of trust towards Ben. How might somebody less sympathetic have responded? Show this as a scene.
2 Suppose two of Giselle's friends, Alfie and Colin (who appear in 'The Diary') barge in as Ben is reading her diary. Show what could happen.
3 Think about the contrast in Giselle's reactions between 'The Diary' and 'Giselle's Diary'. Are there people to whom you would trust your thoughts and others to whom you would not? Discuss what makes the difference.
4 Playing one of the characters in the scene, write an account for your diary of what happened in it. Compare your version with that of the other person in the scene.
5 Write an extract from a diary that you think someone could have written about you.
6 Devise a scene in which you confide something in your best friend, which you have felt unable to tell him or her before.

The Heap

'The Heap' is not a scene – it is a dramatic image, which gives a context to the scenes. This is an account of how it was presented on stage.

You may want to use this first to get an idea how the whole piece looked. Or you may wish to return to it at the end to round off the work.

The play opened with a pile of people on stage. Each person was tumbling over the others. The cast was all clinging and hanging onto a tall ladder. There was a mass of heads, arms, legs and bodies . . . and out of it all came the voices, each one shouting to be heard over the crowd. The lines interrupted one another very fast, with the rhythm and urgency of the flow making each phrase like a different note on a xylophone. It was impossible to distinguish who was speaking which words. It was just a heap of people.

The play closed, too, with 'The Heap' and the same lines were spoken. This time, however, the people stood far apart, spread across the stage. By then the audience knew everyone in the cast and could pick out clearly each one of the personalities as they drew attention to themselves in turn. Everyone in the crowd was calling out for their chance to be heard.

How 'The Heap' can be done

On stage, each of the cast had a couple of lines and everyone was involved. It may suit you to do the same.

Or, here, the lines are numbered 1 to 6. Select half a dozen people and number them 1 to 6, too. Each takes a line as their number comes round.

As the lines are read from the page, they should pile in thick and fast. Very quickly you should achieve the effect of a rowdy crowd. It takes a lot of concentration.

If you want to go as far as learning the lines and putting them into action, the group can find its own physical image to represent the idea. Should the heap of people be facing or turned away from each other? Are they bundled together or far apart reaching for each other?

'The Heap' as background to the scenes

All the cast was on stage all the time, like a living backdrop throughout. During 'Richard on the Floor', for example, the action is about five characters. Sixteen others looked on like a crowd at the spectacle of a street accident. There were 'oohs' and 'ahs' as Richard was floored by Gary. It could be played, as the script here suggests, with the surrounding characters in a school common room or youth club. When 'The Diary' begins Giselle is sitting writing her diary. The stage behind was full of silhouetted people, as though seen through lighted windows – each one half turned away in a secret world writing a diary. During a monologue, while one person faced the audience with their own story, all the others stood confronting the audience too. There was the buzz of everyone's voice, like a muttering crowd, from which the lone voice for the monologue's emerged.

'The Heap', then, like an amoeba changed shape. But it never left the stage. This is why we have included here the few lines which began and finished the play. You may not want to use them alone, but if the script comes together as a production that crowd is central to the structure of the play.

– Listen, I want to tell you this . . . 1
– Let me say it then. Now . . . 2
– No, no, no, listen. Right . . . 3
– Oi, it's my turn to speak . . . 4
– Come on, the way I see it, it's obvious, clear . . . 5
– Listen then . . . 6
– You've had you say. It's my turn now . . . 1
– The point is . . . 2
– I can't tell you if you're not listening . . . 3
– If I had a chance to speak, I'd say millions of things. 4
– Listen to me . . . 5
– I just can't explain . . . 6
– Shh!! 1
– This is important, so let me have my say, eh? 2
– I mean the rubbish you come out with . . . 3
– Shh!! 4
– How should I begin? 5
– The way I see it, right . . . 6
– Just give it a rest for a second . . . 1
– The point is, right . . . the point is . . . 2
– Yes, but . . . no, but . . . 3

– And it's quite clear . . . 4
– Listen I'm telling you this because it's very important to me, right . . . 5
– If I had a chance to speak I'd say millions of things. 6
– I worry that I'll tell you and you won't even be listening . . . 1
– So, right, now . . . 2
– Come on . . . 3
– Why is what I've got to say any less important than what you've been on about? 4
– It's important to me so you should listen . . . 5
– Right, now the point is . . . 6
– How should I begin? 1

Warm-up Notes

These are simple suggestions which may help to warm up a group for work on any of the scenes.

The Diary

In small groups, invent a scene in which someone has found the diary of another friend who is not present. The person who has found the diary has read it and is now revealing what is in it. Work out other people's reactions to that.

A Birthday

A group of friends have been turned away from the club they wanted to go to, because one of them was not allowed in for some reason. Act out the scene on the bus on the way home, when they are all disappointed.

Diannah

(i) Show some scenes in which two people meet at a party.
(ii) Discuss how you might react when someone cries in front of you.

Richard on the Floor

Discuss what being 'on the floor' means, in terms of being beaten. Can you remember a time when you could not stand up for yourself or a time when you helped to 'pick up' someone when they were low.

Natalie Wood

Show a scene in which three friends are watching television. The programme is NOT the main topic of conversation.

Can You Hear Me?

Work in pairs or groups. One person tries to keep a straight face, while the others attempt to make him or her laugh. (No physical contact allowed).

Promotion

Show the dialogue between two friends at work together.

While they are talking keep up the constant activity, which their work demands.

Monologues

This can be used for any of the monologues.

Write what you think could be a page from your diary ten years from now. In it, let us know a little about your life and circumstances.

Giselle's Diary

Invent a scene in which someone gives a present to a friend. How do both people show their feelings?